Editor
Emily R. Smith, M.A. Ed.

Editorial Manager
Elizabeth Morris, Ph.D.

Editor-in-Chief
Sharon Coan, M.S. Ed.

Illustrator
Howard Chaney

Cover Design
Jeff Sutherland

Cover Artist
José Tapia

Photo Credit
Digital Imagery © copyright 2000 Corel, Inc.

Art Coordinator
Denice Adorno

Imaging
Ralph Olmedo, Jr.

Product Manager
Phil Garcia

Published in partnership with
Ready Ed Publications
11/17 Foley Street
Balcatta WA 6021
Australia
www.readyed.com.au

Publishers
Rachelle Cracchiolo, M.S. Ed.
Mary Dupuy Smith, M.S. Ed.

Internet Quests

MY COMMUNITY

Primary

Authors

Jane Bourke and Kell

Teacher Created Materials, Inc.
6421 Industry Way
Westminster, CA 92683
www.teachercreated.com

ISBN-0-7439-3404-4

Table of Contents

Introduction
How to Use This Book . . . 3
Teachers' Notes . . . 4
Internet Activity Pages
Around Your Town . . . 6
Your Neighborhood . . . 7
Visit the Zoo . . . 8
Kids Town . . . 9
Making Our World Better . . . 10
The ABCs of Our Nation . . . 11
What Makes Us Special? . . . 12
How You Can Help . . . 13
Staying Safe . . . 14
Around Your House . . . 15
Use Your Head . . . 16
Staying Safe . . . 17
Danger Around Town . . . 18
Alternet Activity Pages
Our Community . . . 19
Welcome to My Community . . . 20
Getting Around . . . 21
Jobs in the Community . . . 22
Different Families Around the World . . . 23
Joshua's Family . . . 24
Ivona's Family . . . 25
Simon's Family . . . 26
Jordan's Family . . . 27
Thu Lan's Family . . . 28
Environments in Our Community . . . 29
Natural and Man-made Features . . . 30
Different Environments . . . 31
My Time Line . . . 32
General Activity Pages
Who Lives in Our Community? . . . 33
Places in the Community . . . 34
Different Jobs . . . 35
Clothing and Equipment . . . 36
Animals in Their Environments . . . 37
Jobs in Our Community . . . 38
Things to Do . . . 39
Your Week . . . 40
How Do You...? . . . 41
Your Job . . . 42
How Are We Like Others in Our Community? . . . 43
Families . . . 44
Multicultural Community . . . 45
What Do You Think? . . . 46
Answer Key . . . 47

Introduction

How to Use This Book

1. Internet Activity Pages

Note: As this is not an introductory book on using the Internet, you will need to have some understanding of how to navigate the World Wide Web and how to open various Internet addresses prior to attempting these Internet-related activities.

To make use of the pages titled **Internet Activity Pages**, access the *Teacher Created Materials* World Wide Web site at the following address:

http://www.teachercreated.com/books/3404

(Bookmark this site for easy access later.)

When the page opens in your browser, you will see a listing of page numbers and links to Web site addresses. If you click on one of the provided links, you will be taken to the Web page without having to laboriously type the address.

The CD-ROM included with this book also contains hyperlinks that will automatically connect you to the Web sites on the Internet.

2. Alternet Activity Pages

To make use of the pages titled **Alternet Activity Pages**, insert the Alternet CD into your computer's CD-ROM drive. The HTML files on the Alternet CD-ROM require either *Microsoft Internet Explorer* or *Netscape Navigator* to run, so you will need to access one or the other of these browsers. The CD-ROM contains the Alternet package relevant to this book.

The minimum hardware requirement for use of the Alternet program is any computer that uses a frame-capable browser. This includes both Macintosh and Windows operating systems.

3. How to Use the Alternet Program

The Alternet CD can be used on both IBM or Macintosh computers. Although you will need a browser to view the files, the computer does not need to be connected to the Internet, as all files are self-contained.

You may use the files directly from the CD by clicking on the *My Community* folder and then opening the file titled [*begin.htm*]. For faster operation you can copy the contents of the *My Community* folder to a folder on your hard disk, remove the CD for safekeeping, then open [*begin.htm*] on your hard disk.

It is recommended that you create a new folder for the Alternet set from each book you have purchased (*Plants*, *Animals*, etc.). Name the folder after the book you are using.

Note: When you load the Alternet program for your students to use, the browser may give warning messages about connection difficulties. This is because you are not attempting to connect to the Internet. You can ignore this by clicking **OK**.

Note: Purchase of a single book gives you the right to copy the Alternet program on up to ten computers.

Teachers' Notes

Teacher Information

This series is designed to provide teachers of primary-aged children with a multimedia-based set of resources for the *My Community* theme.

In using this multimedia resource, students will be required to learn and utilize a range of associated skills such as:

- reading and interpreting given information.
- summarizing given information.
- using generalizations based on given information.
- navigating around a Web site.

What does the multimedia approach consist of?

This series aims to provide teachers with a three-pronged approach to meeting the requirements of concepts related to scientific research curriculum. It combines the use of traditional information sources such as reference books and materials with the enormous information capabilities of the Internet and the appeal of computer databases as provided by our Alternet program. As many schools face practical limitations in trying to make use of information accessed through the Internet and computer software, the materials provided here are aimed at having the class working as three groups, each using different methods of information retrieval, which eases the pressures on the available hardware and facilities.

1. The Internet:

The use of the related activity pages in this book (titled **Internet Activity Pages**), together with the information sources provided by the World Wide Web, lends a contemporary and exciting aspect to studies in this subject area. As detailed on page 3 of this book, students access the relevant Web pages through the *Teacher Created Materials* Web site and use the information they find to complete the associated tasks on the activity pages.

2. The Alternet Program

The Alternet is a database of information and pictures related to the strand of study on which students are working. Its appearance emulates Web sites found on the Internet's World Wide Web and it is navigated in exactly the same way as the Web through the use of browsers. As with the Internet activities described above, students use the information gathered from the files to complete the relevant activity pages in this book (titled **Alternet Activity Pages**).

3. General Activities

For the activity pages in these sections (titled **General Activity Pages**), students utilize traditional print-related reference materials to complete the tasks on the sheets. It would be useful for a collection of appropriate books to be assembled before commencing the unit so these can be accessed and used with as little disruption as possible. Alternatively, Web site references have been included where possible to provide background information for teachers.

Teachers' Notes *(cont.)*

Updating and Checking of Internet Addresses

The dynamic nature of the Internet means that some sites may change URLs or even disappear altogether. An ongoing role of the publishers will be to monitor changes and post them on our Web site. All addresses used are checked weekly and changes will be posted on our Web site: **http://www.teachercreated.com/books/3404**.

Suggested Use of this Series

As indicated, a multimedia approach has been utilized not only to provide students with a range of reference sources but also to take into account the difficulties schools have in trying to match limited resource access with the requirements of the curriculum. To help teachers plan for these contingencies, this book has been structured to allow units of work where groups rotate from one information source to the next on a week-to-week basis.

It is important to note that the activities in each section are "stand-alone," meaning that students will not need to complete previous activities in order to work successfully. Exactly how teachers choose to use the materials is obviously dependent on the amount of computer hardware and Internet access available, but with a bare minimum in mind, books have been designed to allow a rotation (assuming one period per week is spent on the unit).

To help follow a planning pattern such as this, the following checklist can be used to check off the activity sheets that each group has completed:

1. Where possible, units are evenly balanced as in the example below, i.e., there is an equivalent number of Internet, Alternet, and Print Research activities in each section of the book to allow for easy rotation of groups.
2. Activity pages are designed to take about 25–30 minutes—the approximate length of time usually available in a school period after preliminaries have been sorted out.

Check List

	Groups		
Internet	1	2	3
Your Neighborhood			
Visit the Zoo			
Kids Town			
The ABCs of Our Nation			
What Makes Us Special?			
How You Can Help			
Around Your House			
Use Your Head			
Stay Safe			
Danger Around Town			

	Groups		
Alternet	1	2	3
Welcome to My Community			
Getting Around			
Jobs in the Community			
Joshua's Family			
Ivona's Family			
Simon's Family			
Jordan's Family			
Thu Lan's Family			
Natural and Man-Made Features			
Different Environments			
My Time Line			

	Groups		
General	1	2	3
Places in the Community			
Different Jobs			
Clothing and Equipment			
Animals in Their Environments			
Things to Do			
Your Week			
How Do You . . . ?			
Your Job			
Families			
Multicultural Community			
What Do You Think?			

Around Your Town

Content Area(s):

- reading and comprehension
- social studies
- technology

Objectives:

In this section students:

- navigate Web sites and find required information.
- identify roles of professionals in the community.
- identify animals in different parts of the world.
- find and record information about the state in which they live.
- play "Word Fun" and record the results.

Materials Required:

- computer with Internet access
- pencil or pen

Web Site(s):

- Students need to access the TCM Web page for the *My Community* book at:

http://www.teachercreated.com/books/3404

- Students then click on the link to the page on which they are working.
- Allow the children time to familiarize themselves with the Web site before starting the activity sheets.

Time:

- Approximately 30 minutes per lesson

Teaching Tips and Suggestions:

Your Neighborhood (page 7)

- Students can brainstorm a list of all the places in their community.
- Explain to the students that when the cursor turns into a hand, they can click on links to the buildings.

Visit the Zoo (page 8)

- Talk about the way zoos are organized.
- Although zoos are not part of every local community, they are part of larger communities and are a good place to learn. Ask students what other places in the community are good for learning.
- Talk about the animals that are part of the everyday community.

Kids Town (page 9)

- Explain that there are fifty states in the United States of America and that all states are unique with different flags, characteristics, and state symbols.
- This activity also includes word games and riddles.

Name________________________________

Your Neighborhood

Go to **http://www.teachercreated.com/books/3404**

Click on **Page 7**, **Site 1**

1. Name the six buildings that are shown on the map.

____________________ ____________________ ____________________

____________________ ____________________ ____________________

✏ Click on the **Post Office**

2. Who picks up and brings the mail? ____________________

3. What is your home address? ____________________

✏ Click on the **Fire Station**.

4. What do fire fighters do? ____________________

5. What should you do if there is a fire in your house? ____________________

✏ Click on the **School**.

6. Name three types of people who can help you at school.

____________________ ____________________ ____________________

✏ Click on the **Library**.

7. Name two places where you can find a librarian.

____________________ ____________________

✏ Click on the **Police Station**.

8. Describe two things that police officers do.

____

____

Name ______________________

Visit the Zoo

Go to **http://www.teachercreated.com/books/3404**

Click on **Page 8**, **Site 1**

✏ Animals in zoos are grouped by where they live in nature. Click on **Oceans** at the bottom of the page to learn more about ocean animals.

1. What covers more than two-thirds of the earth's surface? __________

2. What four different animals does this part of the "zoo" tell you about?

__________ __________ __________ __________

✏ Click on **Africa** at the bottom of this site. Answer the questions about African animals.

3. What does an elephant use its trunk for?

____

4. What is the tallest land animal living in the world today?

____

5. What does the word "hippopotamus" mean? __________________

✏ Click on **Australia** at the bottom of the Web site to answer these questions.

6. How does a marsupial mother carry her baby?

____

7. Name two marsupials.

______________ ______________

✏ Click on the **Polar Regions** link at the bottom of this Web page.

8. Caribou are also known as ______________________________.

9. What are two other polar animals? ______________ ______________

Extra! On the back of this sheet, write about what animals are part of your community.

Name______________________________

Kids Town

Go to **http://www.teachercreated.com/books/3404**

Click on **Page 9**, **Site 1**

1. How many places can you visit on the map in Kids Town? ____________

✏ Click on the **Library** and then click on the section of the country that your state is in. Finally, click on your state and fill in the table below.

Write the name of your state in interesting letters in this box.

capital: ______________________	flower: ______________________
induction date: ________________	bird: _________________________
order of induction: ______________	tree: _________________________
nickname: _____________________	song: ________________________

✏ Next, click on the link to the **School** at the bottom of the Web page. Click on **Word Fun** and choose **Easy**. Have fun playing the game!

a. What was the first word you found? ______________________________

b. How many tries did it take you to get the word? ____________________

c. Play again. What was the second word? __________________________

d. How many tries did that word take you? __________________________

✏ Click on **Toy Store** at the bottom of the page. Choose **Riddles** and see how many riddles you can solve. Write the answers on the lines below.

1st ____

2nd ____

3rd ____

Making Our World Better

Content Area(s):

- language
- social studies
- technology

Objectives:

In this section students:

- navigate Web sites and find required information.
- identify some of the characteristics and elements of our nation.
- complete a Web diagram for themselves and another person.
- identify ways to keep their community healthy and help save the environment.

Materials Required:

- computer with Internet access
- pencil or pen

Web Site(s):

- Students need to access the TCM Web page for the *My Community* book at:

http://www.teachercreated.com/books/3404

- Students then click on the link to the page on which they are working.
- Allow the children time to familiarize themselves with the Web site before starting the activity sheets.

Time:

- Approximately 30 minutes per lesson

Teaching Tips and Suggestions:

The ABCs of Our Nation (page 11)

- Some of the words may be difficult for the students so you may want to go over them as a class.
- Have a discussion about what the United States means to them.

What Makes Us Special? (page 12)

- This can be a good classroom community-building activity.
- Discuss the importance of having many different types of people in a community to get all the necessary jobs done.

How You Can Help (page 13)

- Have students discuss what they know about the environment.
- Challenge students to do the suggestions on this Web site for a week and have each student keep a journal of what he or she did and how he or she felt about it.

Name________________________________

The ABCs of Our Nation

Go to **http://www.teachercreated.com/books/3404**

Click on **Page 11**, **Site 1**

✏ Click on each letter that is shown below to find out more about our nation. Use the Web site to discover what each letter stands for and explain it on the lines below. You can click on the small letters at the bottom of each page to go to the next letter.

O is for ________________________________

U is for ________________________________

R is for ________________________________

N is for ________________________________

A is for ________________________________

T is for ________________________________

I is for ________________________________

O again is still for ________________________________

N again is still for ________________________________

Extra! Now write an acrostic like this one for your name on the back of this paper. Use words that describe yourself.

Name ______________________________

What Makes Us Special?

Go to **http://www.teachercreated.com/books/3404**

Click on **Page 12**, **Site 1**

✏ Read "The New Kid in Town" and fill in the blanks below.

1. Each of us has _____________ and _____________ that make us special.

✏ Click on the link for **Before You Read: What Makes Us Special?**

2. Make a web here about your interests.

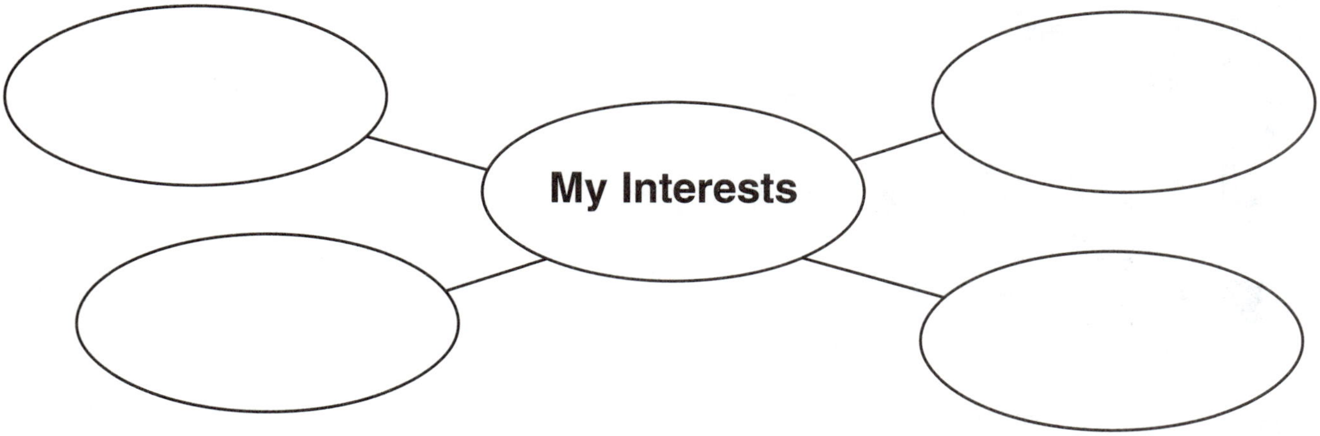

3. Every person in a community is special. Share your web with a friend and make one for his or her interests.

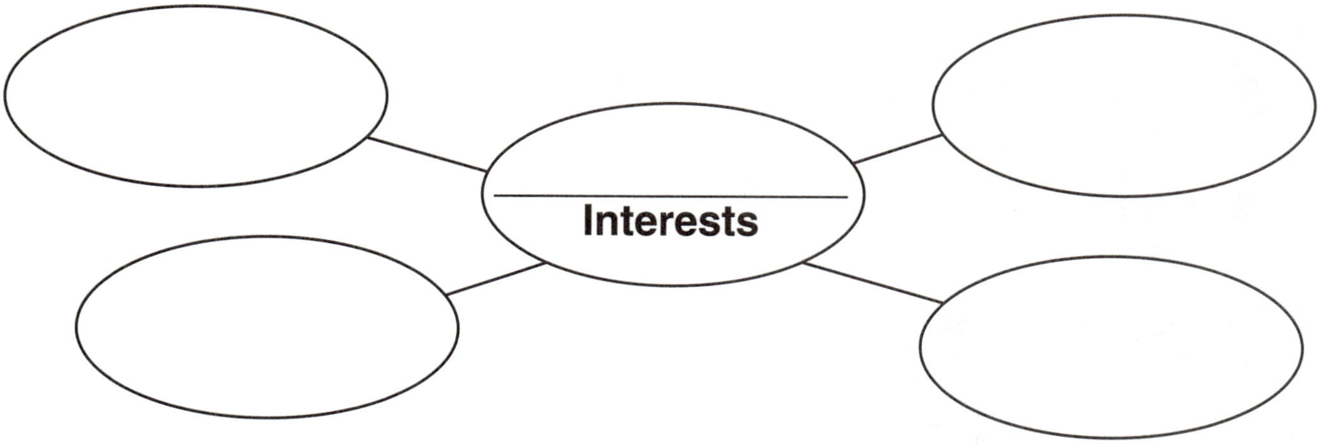

Extra! Explore some of the other links on this page.

Name ______________________________

How You Can Help

Go to **http://www.teachercreated.com/books/3404**

Click on **Page 13**, **Site 1**

✏ Click on each of the number cards on the Web site to see the secret message about how you can help keep your community healthy and save the environment. After reading the information, answer the questions below.

1. Card number one says that you should

   ________________________________.

2. What can you do with trash and recyclables?

   ____

3. What should you do when you leave a room?

   ____

4. What is the right thing to do at school, at home, at the park, and everywhere you go?

   ____

5. How can you help Earth stay clean?

   ____

6. What keeps going and going? ________________

7. What should you do sometimes instead of riding in a car? ________________

8. What should you do when you are brushing your teeth?

   ____

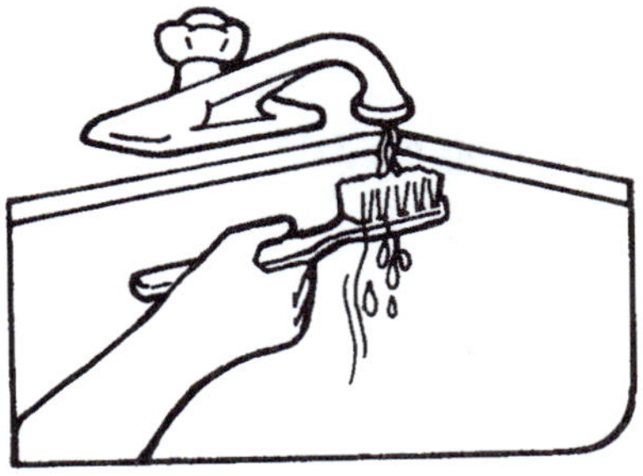

9. How can you save half the amount of water you use?

   ____

10. What should you cut so that fish and other animals do not get caught in them?

    ____

Extra! Check out some of the links to this site. They are GREAT!

Staying Safe

Content Area(s):

- reading and comprehension
- social studies
- technology

Objectives:

In this section students:

- navigate Web sites and find required information.
- identify dangerous chemicals in each part of a house.
- read a story and answer questions about safety.
- print a coloring page from a Web site.
- read and answer questions on safety suggestions in many situations.

Materials Required:

- computer with Internet access
- pencil or pen

Web Site(s):

- Students need to access the TCM Web page for the *My Community* book at:

http://www.teachercreated.com/books/3404

- Students then click on the link to the page on which they are working.
- Allow the children time to familiarize themselves with the Web site before starting the activity sheets.

Time:

- Approximately 30 minutes per lesson

Teaching Tips and Suggestions:

Around Your House (page 15)

- Explain that the cursor will change into a hand and a text box will pop up to tell students about each item in the rooms.
- Do a poison control lesson.

Use Your Head (page 16)

- Extend the lesson to discuss more cycling safety issues.

Stay Safe (page 17)

- There are several sections to this Web site with valuable safety suggestions.

Danger Around Town (page 18)

- This is a strong reminder about how to watch out for dangers around town.
- Extend these activities by bringing in speakers to share their ideas with the class.

Name________________________________

Around Your House

Go to **http://www.teachercreated.com/books/3404**

Click on **Page 15**, **Site 1**

✏ At the Web site, click on each room in the house. Move the cursor around the room until the arrow looks like a hand and then stop. The name of the object will show up in a little box near the hand. Decide whether or not the object is poisonous or toxic. If you need more information, click on the object to find out about it.

1. Name at least three dangerous chemicals in the garage. ________________

____

2. Name three toxic chemicals in the cellar or laundry room. ________________

____

3. What are four dangerous things in the kitchen? ________________

____

4. The living room is pretty safe, but what two dangers are there?

____

5. The dangerous chemicals in the bedroom are kind of tricky. Can you find both of them?

____

____

6. The bathroom has four dangerous chemicals. Can you name two of them?

____

7. Now, take a look at what you might find in the backyard. Name two dangerous chemicals there.

____

Name ______________________

Use Your Head

Go to **http://www.teachercreated.com/books/3404**
Click on **Page 16**, **Site 1**

✏ Click on the arrow to move to the next page of the story. If there is no arrow, click on the picture to fix what is wrong.

1. What do Elmo and Teddy need to find before they can ride the bike to the park?

____

2. What does Elmo need to do before he crosses the street?

____

3. What do you do before you cross the street? ______________________________

____

4. How is a helmet different from a hat? ______________________________

____

5. What are some other times you need to wear a helmet? ______________________________

____

✏ Click on link for **More Safe Cruising** below the last story in the picture. Then click on **Just for Kids**. Finally, click on the **Print Me** activity and **Coloring Pages** link.

6. Name four of the coloring pages that help you remember how to be safe.

____

____

____

____

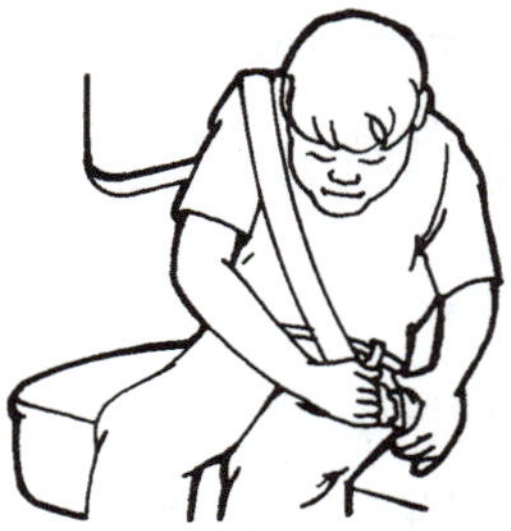

Extra! Get your teacher's permission to print one of the pages to color!

Name______________________________

Stay Safe

Go to **http://www.teachercreated.com/books/3404**

Click on **Page 17**, **Site 1**

This site will help you with ideas about how to stay safe in your community.

✏ Answer the questions below by clicking the arrows on the Web site.

1. What are some things you should do after an accident? ______________

    ____

2. Name two rules for safety on wheels. ____________________________

    ____

3. What is something you can do when a bully picks on you? ____________

    ____

4. How do you call for help in an emergency?

    ____

    ____

5. What should you do if you find a knife, gun, or weapon? Circle either **True** or **False** in each statement below.

Pick up the weapon and take it to an adult.	**True**	**False**
Leave the weapon alone and find an adult you trust.	**True**	**False**
Call 9-1-1 if you can't find an adult nearby.	**True**	**False**

6. How can you stay safe in parks and play areas? ____________________

    ____

Extra! On the back of this page, draw or write other things you learned about staying safe.

Name ____________________

Danger Around Town

Go to **http://www.teachercreated.com/books/3404**

Click on **Page 18**, **Site 1**

✏ Carefully follow the instructions on the Web site. Your radar is your ability to see danger. Click on the danger spots on the Web site to learn more about the problem.

On the lines below, write eight of the ten dangers you need to watch out for around town.

1. ____________________
2. ____________________
3. ____________________
4. ____________________
5. ____________________
6. ____________________
7. ____________________
8. ____________________

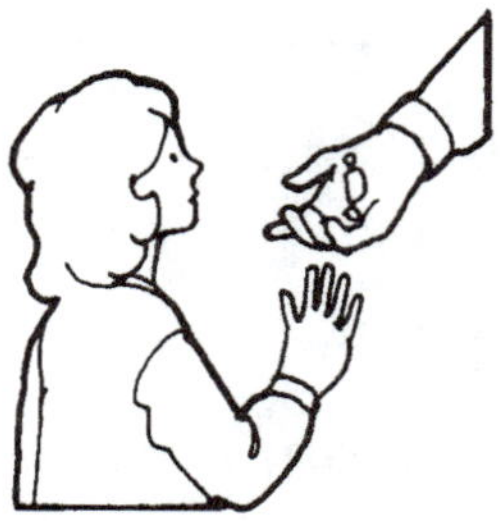

Extra! Write down any other things that you know to stay safe around your house, your school, or your town.

____

____

____

____

____

____

Our Community

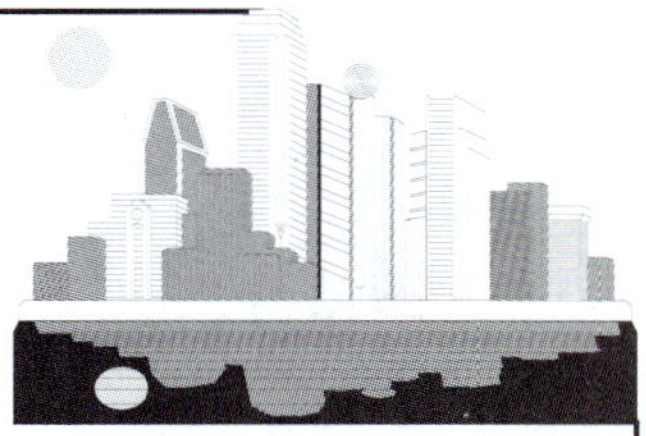

Content Area(s):

- reading and comprehension
- social studies
- technology

Objectives:

In this section students:

- navigate around Alternet sites and find required information.
- identify elements and features of a city and a town.
- create a graph showing how people travel to school.
- fill in a table comparing different jobs in the community.

Materials Required:

- computer with Internet browser
- Alternet CD-ROM
- pencil or pen

Alternet:

- To use the Alternet CD-ROM, open [*begin.htm*]. For more instructions see the section titled *How to Use the Alternet Program* on page 3.
- To go to individual pages, students access the index page and then click on the number of the page they are using.

Time:

- Approximately 30 minutes per lesson

Teaching Tips and Suggestions:

Welcome to My Community (page 20)

- Explain that every community has aspects that are like and different from other communities.

Getting Around (page 21)

- Preview how to create a graph and how to read and record information on a graph.

Jobs in the Community (page 22)

- Explain that students will have to pay attention to each person's job to fill in all of the blanks in the table.
- Have parents of the students in your class come in and talk about their jobs and the community.

Name ______________________________

Welcome to My Community

For this activity you will need the **My Community Alternet CD-ROM**. Click on the link to **Page 20**.

✏ Explore the links on the site and then answer the questions below.

1. Circle the items that you would be able to **buy** in Smartville.

tomatoes	movie ticket
gas	milk
medicine	surfboard
furniture	magazine
house	new car
basketball	bicycle

2. Circle the things that you would be able to **do** in Smartville.

go to a movie	fly a kite
catch a train	eat Chinese food
play tennis	stay in a five-star hotel
catch a plane	take a taxi

3. How is Smartville the same as your community?

____

____

4. How is Smartville different from your community?

____

____

5. How is a big city different from a small town?

____

____

____

____

Name________________________________

Getting Around

For this activity you will need the **My Community Alternet CD-ROM**.

Click on the link to **Page 21**.

✏ Explore the links on the site and then answer the questions below.

1. What types of transportation can people in Smartville use?

____

____

2. What types of transportation do you have in your community?

____

____

Graphing Activity

✏ Show the number of children in your class who have:

traveled to school by **bus** 	
traveled to school by **bicycle** 	
traveled on a **train** 	
traveled on a **boat** 	
traveled in a **taxi** 	

Name ______________________________

Jobs in the Community

For this activity you will need the **My Community Alternet CD-ROM**.

Click on the link to **Page 22**.

✏ Complete the table to describe some different jobs in the community. Draw a picture of each worker under the job's name.

Job	Special Skills	Equipment	How do they help us?
mechanic	They train on the job and learn all about engines.	wrenches, overalls	They fix our cars, trucks, motorcycles, and boats.
doctor			
P.E. teacher			
bookstore owner			
mail delivery person			
construction worker			

Different Families Around the World

Content Area(s):

- reading and comprehension
- social studies
- technology

Objectives:

In this section students:

- navigate around Alternet sites and find required information.
- explore different family groups and families from diverse backgrounds.
- identify similarities and differences among various cultural groups.
- compare their lives to others.

Materials Required:

- computer with Internet browser
- Alternet CD-ROM
- pencil or pen

Alternet:

- To use the Alternet CD-ROM, open [*begin.htm*]. For more instructions see the section titled *How to Use the Alternet Program* on page 3.
- To go to individual pages, students access the index page and then click on the number of the page they are using.

Time:

- Approximately 30 minutes per lesson

Teaching Tips and Suggestions:

- For this section of the Alternet, you may want to create a world map bulletin board so your students can locate various areas of the world as they learn about them.
- Have students write stories or draw to show what their families are like.
- Create a class book with students depicting the different types of families and cultures in their classroom and school. Extend this concept into an appreciation of differences and values of all.
- You may choose to have different groups do different families and then share what they found and what they thought.

Name ______________________________

Joshua's Family

For this activity you will need the **My Community Alternet CD-ROM**.

Click on the link to **Page 24**.

✏ Read all about Joshua's family on the site.

1. How is Joshua's family like your family?

____

____

____

____

2. How is his family different from your family?

____

____

____

____

3. What does Joshua do in his spare time?

____

____

4. Describe what you do in your spare time. Then draw a picture of yourself doing your favorite activity.

____

____

____

____

Name______________________________

Ivona's Family

For this activity you will need the **My Community Alternet CD-ROM**.

Click on the link to **Page 25**.

1. What country does Ivona's family come from?______________________________
2. Color Ivona's country on this map.
3. What is the population? ______________
4. What is its capital city? ______________
5. Name the people in Ivona's family.

   ____

   ____

6. Why do you think this family moved from their home country?

   ____

   ____

7. What is an immigrant? ____

   ____

8. What problems might Ivona's family have faced by moving here?

   ____

   ____

9. Why is it important that her family remember how to speak Romanian?

   ____

   ____

Name ______________________________

Simon's Family

For this activity you will need the **My Community Alternet CD-ROM**.

Click on the link to **Page 26**.

✏ Read all about Simon's family on the site.

1. Who are the people that make up Simon's family?

____

____

2. In what ways is Simon's family the same as and different from yours? Fill in the table.

Same	Different

3. Some children receive an allowance from their parents. How does Simon earn his money? ______________________________

✏ Draw some other ways you could make pocket money.

Name______________________________

Jordan's Family

For this activity you will need the **My Community Alternet CD-ROM**.

Click on the link to **Page 27**.

✏ Read all about Jordan's family on the site.

1. Who are the people that make up Jordan's family?

____

____

2. How is Jordan's family different from your family?

____

____

____

Celebrating Holidays

3. How does Jordan celebrate Christmas?

____

____

____

4. Draw your family celebrating a special day. Write a sentence or two explaining your picture.

____

____

____

____

____

Name ______________________

Thu Lan's Family

For this activity you will need the **My Community Alternet CD-ROM**.
Click on the link to **Page 28**.

1. What country does Thu Lan's family come from? ______________________
2. Color her home country on this map.

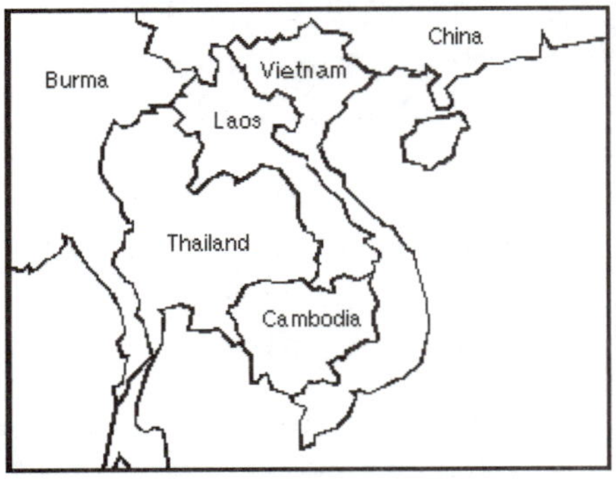

3. What is the population? ______________________
4. What is its capital city? ______________________
5. What types of food do the people eat?

____

____

6. What does Thu Lan do after school?

____

7. What do you do after school? ______________________

____

Celebrating Holidays

8. Draw a picture and write three things about how Thu Lan celebrates the New Year.

a. ______________________

____

b. ______________________

____

c. ______________________

____

Environments in Our Community

Content Area(s):

- reading and comprehension
- social studies
- technology

Objectives:

In this section students:

- navigate around Alternet sites and find required information.
- differentiate between natural and man-made features.
- describe three different types of environments
- identify cultures with environments.
- create a time line of their lives.

Materials Required:

- computer with Internet browser
- Alternet CD-ROM
- pencil or pen

Alternet:

- To use the Alternet CD-ROM, open [*begin.htm*]. For more instructions see the section titled *How to Use the Alternet Program* on page 3.
- To go to individual pages, students access the index page and then click on the number of the page they are using.

Time:

- Approximately 30 minutes per lesson

Teaching Tips and Suggestions:

Natural and Man-made Features (page 30)

- Make sure that students understand what an environment is.
- Create murals or collages with magazine pictures of natural and man-made features.

Different Environments (page 31)

- Introduce that climate is the general weather patterns of an area.
- Discuss how weather or climate affects an environment (food, housing, farming, animals, clothing, etc.). Have students brainstorm different types of environments.

My Time Line (page 32)

- Preview time lines with the students. Use your life to model how to make a time line.

Name ______________________________

Natural and Man-made Features

For this activity you will need the **My Community Alternet CD-ROM**.
Click on the link to **Page 30**.

✏ Look at the two photos on the Alternet site.

1. Describe the city environment.

____

____

2. List the natural things in the city photo.

______________ ______________ ______________ ______________

3. List the man-made things in the city photo.

______________ ______________ ______________ ______________

4. Describe the photo of the rural environment.

____

5. List the natural things in the rural photo.

______________ ______________ ______________ ______________

6. List the man-made things in the rural photo.

______________ ______________ ______________ ______________

7. Look out the window of your classroom. List four man-made objects you see.

______________ ______________

______________ ______________

8. List four natural objects you see.

______________ ______________

______________ ______________

Name________________________________

Different Environments

For this activity you will need the **My Community Alternet CD-ROM**.

Click on the link to **Page 31**.

✏ Explore the different types of environments on the Alternet site.

1. What things are part of an environment?

____

____

2. Name and describe three of the environments from the site.

   a. ______________________________________

   ____

   b. ______________________________________

   ____

   c. ______________________________________

   ____

3. Describe the environment that you live in. ______________________

____

____

Draw a person in a hot environment

Draw a person in a cold environment

Name ______________________________

My Time Line

For this activity you will need the **My Community Alternet CD-ROM**.

Click on the link to **Page 32**.

✏ Study Ben's time line using the Alternet site.

Make a time line of your own. Draw pictures or write sentences to show the important things that have happened in your life. Be sure to label the boxes. (You may need to ask someone in your family to help you.)

I was born on ______________________

Years

0

1

2

3

4

5

6

7

8

9

Who Lives in Our Community?

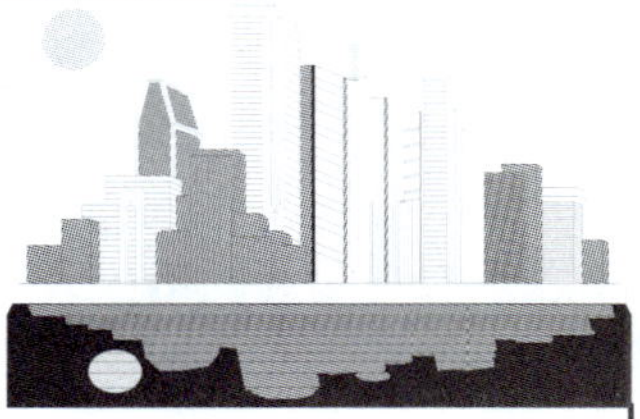

Content Area(s):

- map reading and identification
- social studies
- research

Objectives:

In this section students:

- identify, locate, and use resource materials to find required information.
- identify different places in the community.
- identify country and city jobs and equipment for various jobs.
- research and record information about animals from different environments.

Materials Required:

- library, computer, and other resource materials
- pencil or pen; crayons

Time:

- Approximately 30 minutes per lesson

Teaching Tips and Suggestions:

Places in the Community (page 34)

- Talk about your community. You may choose to have students use graph paper to create a map of a central area of their community or of the school's neighborhood.

Different Jobs (page 35)

- Make sure that students understand the different types of work that are done in the country and in the city. Extend this to have them write or discuss where they would rather live and why.
- Point out to students that there are little boxes in the upper, right-hand corners of each picture in which to put the correct letter.

Clothing and Equipment (page 36)

- Different jobs and environments require different clothing and equipment. Have children talk about how their parents dress for work or describe the different equipment that they use. What clothing and equipment do the students use for their "jobs"?

Animals in Their Environments (page 37)

- Help children decide how to find the necessary information.

Name ______________________________

Places in the Community

Welcome to Smartville!

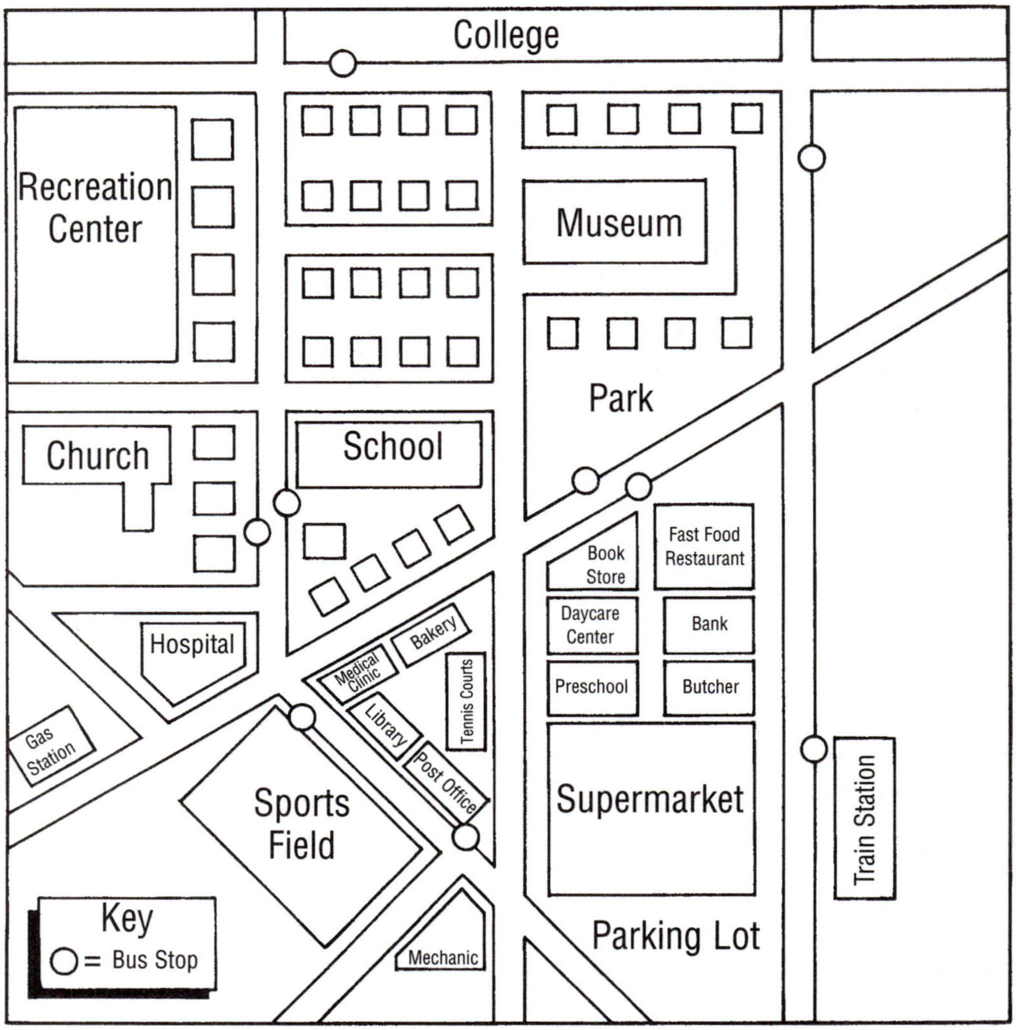

- Color the places you go for your **health** red.
- Color the places you go for **food** green.
- Color the places you go to play **sports or games** yellow.
- Color the places you go to **learn** blue.

What are some other places in this community?

____

____

Name______________________________

Different Jobs

- ✏ Put a **T** next to the jobs that people would do in a small town.
- ✏ Put a **C** next to jobs that people would do in a city.
- ✏ Put a **B** (for both) next to jobs that could be done in either a city or a small town.

 baker	 sheep herder	 miner	 butcher
 grocer	 teacher	 fire fighter	 parking inspector
 doctor	 police officer	 jeweler	 news person
 nurse	 timber worker	 pilot	 train driver
 mechanic	 farmer	 bus driver	 travel agent

Name ______________________________

Clothing and Equipment

✏ Draw a line from the job to the clothing and equipment that the person would need.

scientist

A

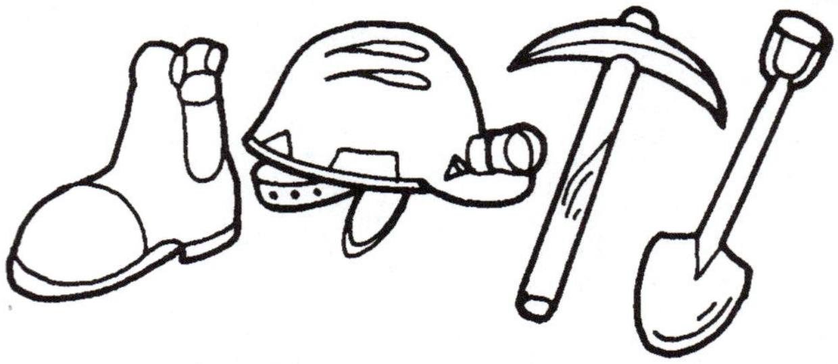

explorer in the desert

B

miner

C

scuba diver

D

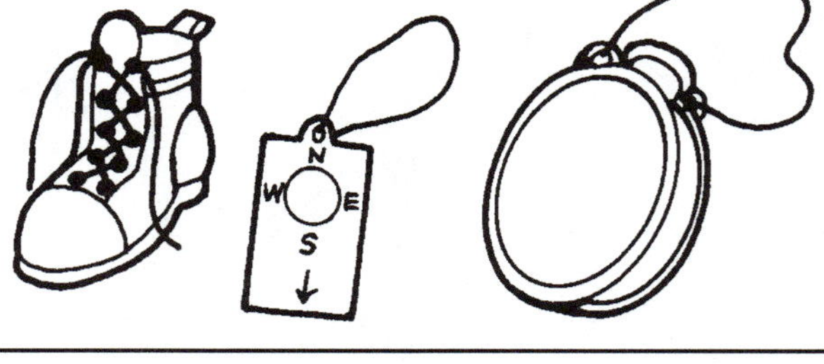

astronaut

E

Name________________________________

Animals in Their Environments

✏ Animals live in different environments. Research these animals to find out how they survive in their environments.

penguin

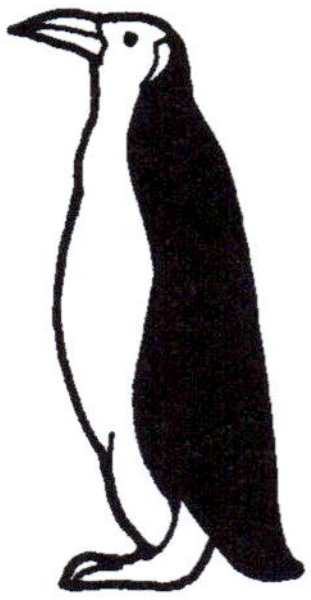

The penguin lives in a(n) __________ environment.

It eats ______________________________

It moves ______________________________

It protects itself by ______________________________

____

lion

The lion lives in a(n) __________ environment.

It eats ______________________________

It moves ______________________________

It protects itself by ______________________________

____

dolphin

The dolphin lives in a(n) __________ environment.

It eats ______________________________

It moves ______________________________

It protects itself by ______________________________

____

An animal that lives near you

This animal lives in a(n) __________ environment.

It eats ______________________________

It moves ______________________________

It protects itself by ______________________________

____

Jobs in Our Community

Content Area(s):

- language
- social studies
- research

Objectives:

In this section students:

- identify, locate, and use resource materials to find required information.
- identify where they go for certain goods and services in the community.
- create schedules for their week.
- answer questions about professions or jobs they would like to do as adults.

Materials Required:

- library, computer, and other resource materials
- pencil or pen; crayons

Time:

- Approximately 30 minutes per lesson

Teaching Tips and Suggestions:

Things to Do (page 39)

- Point out to students that there are little boxes in the upper, right-hand corners of each picture in which to put the correct letter.

Your Week (page 40)

- Explain that many people have schedules or plans that they use to get everything done during the week. Have each student create a schedule of his or her usual week during school. Show an example on the board or overhead. Encourage students to each make space to record reading, playing outside, doing chores, and spending time with friends and family.

How Do You . . . ? (page 41)

- Explain that the pictures don't have to be perfect. This activity can also be linked to teaching students about valuing diversity.

Your Job (page 42)

- Brainstorm with the students and list different jobs in your community. Post each child's job sheet and have him or her dress up and present what he or she knows about that job.

Name________________________________

Things to Do

- Put **Y** (for yes) in the box for the places that you can go in your community.
- Put **V** (for visit) in the box for places you have gone when you were visiting other communities.
- Put **W** (for wish) if it is someplace you would like to go someday.

- Draw a picture of you in:

the city

the country

- In your community, where would you go for the following things?

a haircut: ________________________________

to have your teeth checked: ________________________________

to go swimming: ________________________________

to put gas in the car: ________________________________

to have an operation: ________________________________

Name ______________________________

Your Week

People in a community do different things during the week to make sure that everything goes smoothly. Make a weekly schedule for yourself. Get started by filling in the times that you are at school, the times you do your chores, and when you have sports or music lessons. Then keep track of your free time for a week.

	Mon.	Tues.	Wed.	Thurs.	Fri.	Sat.	Sun.
7:00 A.M.							
8:00 A.M.							
9:00 A.M.							
10:00 A.M.							
11:00 A.M.							
12:00 P.M.							
1:00 P.M.							
2:00 P.M.							
3:00 P.M.							
4:00 P.M.							
5:00 P.M.							
6:00 P.M.							
7:00 P.M.							
8:00 P.M.							
9:00 P.M.							

Name______________________________

How Do You . . . ?

✏ In the boxes, draw how you and your family do the following things.

buy food	go places	cook food
pay for bills	stay warm and dry	have fun
go on vacation	stay healthy	celebrate holidays

Challenge: Not all people do things the same way. Look at some other people's pictures to see if they do things in the same way or in a different way from you and your family.

Name ______________________________

Your Job

✏ Draw the job you would like to have when you are grown up.

1. Why do you think you would like this job?

____

____

____

____

____

2. List some of the special skills you will need.

____

____

____

3. What sort of clothing will you need for this job?

____

____

4. If you could find someone who has this job, what are four questions you might ask him or her?

   a. ____

   b. ____

   c. ____

   d. ____

How Are We Like Others in Our Community?

Content Area(s):

- writing
- social studies
- research

Objectives:

In this section students:

- identify, locate, and use resource materials to find required information.
- write stories about their families.
- compare and contrast themselves to their friends.
- create a chart showing the different places from which people in the class come.
- reflect on learning.

Materials Required:

- library, computer, and other resource materials
- pencil or pen; crayons

Time:

- Approximately 30 minutes per lesson

Teaching Tips and Suggestions:

Families (page 44)

- Have students share stories and facts about their families in small groups.

Multicultural Community (page 45)

- Find and list on the board, all of the foreign countries or regions of the United States from which the students in your class come.

What Do You Think? (page 46)

- Discuss with the students what "reflecting on learning" means. Have a class discussion about the types of things they have learned about their homes, community, state, and country.
- This is a great form of closure to the unit and beneficial for assessment.

Name ______________________

Families

✏ Talk to your friends and students in your class to find out what their families do for fun.

1. Name three things that your family does for fun.

____

____

____

2. What things do other families do the same as your family?

____

____

3. What things do they do differently?

____

____

____

____

____

4. Draw your family and write a story about them. Use the back of the paper if needed.

____

____

____

____

____

Name______________________________

Multicultural Community

✏ People in the United States come from all different places. They are alike in some ways and different in other ways.

1. In what ways are you the same as your friends?

____

____

____

2. How are you different from your friends?

____

____

3. List some ways that people who come from different places are different from you.

____

____

____

✏ Find where each student in your class was born. Put one mark for each student born in the following countries.

Country	Number of Students	Total
United States		
Mexico		

Extra! Make another tally showing where each student's parents were born.

Name ______________________________

What Do You Think?

✏ Thinking about what you have learned and how you learn can help you learn even more. Choose some of the questions below to answer and share what you think about this unit on learning about your community.

- What have you learned about your community and other communities?
- What did you like about this unit of study? What did you dislike? Why?
- What sorts of things can you do to make your community a great place to live?
- How are families different? Why is difference a good thing?

Answer Key

Page 7—Your Neighborhood
1. post office, fire station, school, police station, hospital, library; 2. letter carrier; 3. Answers will vary; 4. They put out fires and respond to emergencies; 5. Get out, meet your family where it is safe, call 9-1-1; 6. teacher, principal, guidance counselor, teacher's aide, nurse, librarian; 7. school and public libraries; 8. They keep neighborhoods safe, make sure people follow rules, direct traffic, and/or solve crimes.

Page 8—Visit the Zoo
1. water; 2. crabs, seahorses, sharks, and starfish; 3. to eat and drink; 4. giraffe; 5. "horse of the river"; 6. in a pouch on her stomach; 7. kangaroo and koala; 8. reindeer; 9. wolf, polar bear, or hare.

Page 9—Kids Town
Answers will vary.

Page 11—The ABCs of Our Nation
O=oath, U=United States of America, R=rights, N=national anthem, A=armed forces, T=tax, I=independence, O=oath, N=national anthem.

Page 12—What Makes Us Special?
Answers will vary.

Page 13—How You Can Help
1. play outside; 2. make crafts; 3. turn off the lights; 4. pick up trash; 5. plant things; 6. rechargeable batteries; 7. walk or ride a bike; 8. turn off the water; 9. take a quick shower instead of a bath; 10. six-pack beverage container rings.

Page 15—Around Your House
Answers will vary.

Page 16—Use Your Head
1. helmets; 2. hold an adult's hand; 3. Answers will vary; 4. it protects the brain from injury; 5-6. Answers will vary.

Page 17—Stay Safe
1. remain calm, find an adult, call 9-1-1 and state the problem and wait for instructions; 2. Answers will vary; 3. Answers will vary; 4. Dial 9-1-1 or "0" for operator. State the problem briefly. Give your full name and address. Remain on the telephone. Don't hang up until you are told to do so; 5. false, true, true; 6. play in groups, follow rules, watch out for glass and other dangers, don't chase balls out into the street, and let your parents know where you are going to be.

Page 18—Danger Around Town
In any order: 1. don't stand too close to strangers; 2. don't get into a car with a stranger; 3. don't take shortcuts through dark places by yourself; 4. don't let strangers take your photo; 5. don't go into buildings with strangers; 6. don't run out into the street without looking both ways; 7. don't cross between two parked cars; 8. pay attention when crossing the road.

Page 20—Welcome to My Community
1. tomatoes, gas, medicine, furniture, house, basketball, movie ticket, milk, magazine, new car, and bicycle; 2. go to a movie, catch a train, play tennis, fly a kite, eat Chinese food, and take a taxi; 3-5. Answers will vary.

Page 21—Getting Around
1. walk, bus, cars, trains; 2. Answers will vary.

Page 22—Jobs in the Community
Answers will vary.

Page 24—Joshua's Family
1-2. Answers will vary; 3. plays sports, meets with friends, watches cows being milked, plays on the farm, etc.; 4. Answers will vary.

Page 25—Ivona's Family
1. Romania; 3. 22,400,000; 4. Bucharest; 5. her dad, mom, and little brother Remy; 6. Answers will vary; 7. a person born in one country who move to another to start a new life; 8. Answers will vary; 9. They hope to go back to Romania someday.

Page 26—Simon's Family
1. his mom, grandma, dad, stepmother, and half sister; 2. Answers will vary; 3. collects recycling bottles.

Answer Key *(cont.)*

Page 27—Jordan's Family
1. his mom, dad, two younger sisters, older brother, and two adult cousins; 2. Answers will vary; 3. Everyone comes to his family's house to play games and make crafts and goodies; 4. Answers will vary.

Page 28—Thu Lan's Family
1. Vietnam; 3. 77 million; 4. Hanoi; 5. fish, rice, and vegetables; 6. She helps her mother at the restaurant.; 7-8. Answers will vary.

Page 30—Natural and Man-made Features
Answers will vary.

Page 31—Different Environments
1. all living and non-living things that surround us; 2. Vietnamese-hot and wet environment, Eskimos-icy cold environment, Native Americans-hot and dry environment, Aborigines-hot and dry environment, Russians-cold and dry environment; 3. Answers will vary.

Page 32—My Time Line
Answers will vary.

Pages 34-35—General Activity Pages
Answers will vary.

Page 36—Clothing and Equipment
scientist-B; explorer-D; miner-A; scuba diver-E; astronaut-C.

Page 37—Animals in Their Environments
Answers will vary.

Page 39–46—General Activity Pages
Answers will vary.